FRANCHISING IN ZAMBIA 2014

Legal and Business Considerations

KENDAL H. TYRE, JR., EXECUTIVE EDITOR
DIANA VILMENAY-HAMMOND, MANAGING EDITOR
COURTNEY L. LINDSAY, II, ASSISTANT EDITOR

LexNoir Foundation

FIRST QUARTER 2014

LexNoir Foundation is the charitable, educational arm of LexNoir, an international network of lawyers connecting the African Diaspora.

This publication, *Franchising in Zambia 2014: Legal and Business Considerations*, contains excerpts from *Franchising in Africa 2014: Legal and Business Considerations*. Both works are published by LexNoir Foundation and reflect the points of view of the authors and editors as of the date of publication and do not necessarily represent the opinions, interpretations, or positions of the law firms or organizations with which they are affiliated, nor the opinions, interpretations or positions of LexNoir Foundation or LexNoir.

Nothing contained in this book is to be considered as the rendering of legal advice, either generally or in connection with any specific issues or case. Readers are responsible for obtaining advice from their own legal counsel or other professional. This book, any forms and agreements or other information herein are intended for educational and informational purposes only.

Table of Contents

Franchising in Zambia

Mabvuto Sakala
Corpus Legal Practitioners

Bibliography of International Franchise Resources

Kendal H. Tyre, Jr., Diana Vilmenay-Hammond, Pierce Haesung Han, Courtney L. Lindsay, II, and Keri McWilliams
Nixon Peabody LLP

Acknowledgment

This book could not have been written without the hard work and dedication of each of the contributing authors and editors. Thank you.

We would like to acknowledge and extend our heartfelt gratitude to Michael Collier and Maria Stallings of the Washington, D.C. office of Nixon Peabody LLP for their invaluable assistance in revising, proofing, and editing this publication.

About the Editors and Authors

Kendal H. Tyre, Jr. – Kendal is a partner in the Washington, D.C. office of Nixon Peabody LLP. He handles domestic and cross-border transactions, including mergers and acquisitions, joint ventures, strategic alliances, licensing, and franchise matters.

In his franchise and licensing practice, Kendal counsels domestic and international franchisors, franchisees, licensors, licensees and distributors regarding U.S. state and federal franchise laws as well as foreign franchise legislation in a variety of jurisdictions. Kendal drafts and provides advice with regard to franchise and license agreements, disclosure documents and area development agreements and has extensive experience drafting and negotiating a variety of other commercial agreements. His client base spans the United States and foreign countries, including South Africa, Kenya, and the United Kingdom.

Kendal is a frequent contributor to franchise publications and a frequent speaker at franchise programs held by the American Bar Association Forum on Franchising and the International Franchise Association.

Kendal is co-chair of the firm's Diversity Action Committee and its Africa Group. Kendal is also the executive director of LexNoir Foundation.

E-mail address: ktyre@nixonpeabody.com

Diana Vilmenay-Hammond – Diana is an attorney in the Washington, D.C. office of Nixon Peabody LLP. She is a member of the firm's Franchise & Distribution Team.

In her franchise practice, Diana works with domestic and international franchisors on transactional and litigation matters. Specifically, she counsels franchisor clients regarding state and federal franchise laws, disclosure and registration obligations.

Diana drafts and negotiates various commercial agreements, including international franchise and development agreements.

Diana has co-authored numerous articles on franchising and frequently co-hosted the Nixon Peabody franchise law webinar series. Topics have included:

- "Franchise Case Law Round-Up: Implications for Your Franchise," February 15, 2012;
- "Social Media Part II: Best Practices in Protecting Your Brand in the New Media," September 14, 2010; and
- "The Awuah Case: Bellwether or Outlier," May 11, 2010

Diana received her J.D. from Howard University School of Law and her B.A. from Georgetown University. She is a member of the American Bar Association (Forum on Franchising).

Email address: dvilmenay@nixonpeabody.com

Pierce Haesung Han – Pierce is an associate in Nixon Peabody's Global Business & Transactions Group. Pierce focuses his practice on three main areas, assisting clients with a variety of complex business transactions.

- Mergers & Acquisitions: Providing assistance to both public and private clients with various mergers and acquisitions, performing due diligence, drafting and negotiating transaction documents, and facilitating closing and post-closing mechanics.
- International Commercial Transactions: Drafting and negotiating a variety of commercial agreements, including international franchise and development agreements, license agreements, and purchase and sale agreements.
- Federal Securities Law Matters: Assisting public and private clients regarding federal securities laws and stock exchange rules relating to corporate governance and disclosure.

Pierce serves as the Secretary of the Asian Pacific Bar Association Educational Fund (an affiliate of the Asian Pacific American Bar Association of the Greater Washington, D.C. Area).

Pierce received his J.D. from Georgetown University Law Center and his B.A. from Case Western Reserve University. He is admitted to practice in the State of New York and the District of Columbia.

E-mail address: phan@nixonpeabody.com

Courtney L. Lindsay, II – Courtney is an associate in Nixon Peabody's Corporate and Finance practice. In his corporate practice, Courtney assists for-profit and non-profit entities with transactional matters and corporate governance. In various capacities, Courtney has been involved in multiple merger and acquisition transactions, including drafting and managing due diligence.

Previously, Courtney worked in the legal and business affairs department at a national cable network, where he handled matters related to the network's LLC agreement, including drafting board and member consent agreements.

Courtney received his J.D. from the University of Virginia School of Law and his B.A. from the University of Virginia. He is admitted to practice in the Commonwealth of Virginia and the District of Columbia.

E-mail address: clindsay@nixonpeabody.com

Keri McWilliams – Keri is an associate in the Franchise & Distribution team of Nixon Peabody LLP. Keri works with clients on a number of franchising issues, including obtaining and maintaining franchise registrations in various states, responding to state inquiries regarding trade practices, ongoing compliance with state and federal regulations, and updating franchise disclosure documents. She also handles franchise sales counseling and franchise system issues.

Keri is a member of the American Bar Association's Forum on Franchising, and the Federal and Minnesota State bar associations. She is also a member of Minnesota Women Lawyers and the Minnesota Association of Black Lawyers, and a volunteer in the Volunteer Lawyers Network.

Keri received her J.D. from the Georgetown University Law Center and her B.F.A. from Washington University. She is admitted to practice in the District of Columbia and Minnesota.

E-mail address: kmcwilliams@nixonpeabody.com

Mabvuto Sakala – Mabvuto is a lecturer of law at the University of Zambia and also a private legal practitioner and partner at Corpus Legal Practitioners in Lusaka, Zambia. His academic and research work with the university is geared towards commercial subjects. Mabvuto's work as a legal practitioner covers a wide range of legal matters including those involving alternative dispute resolution, arbitration and mediation, and business and commercial litigation. He also heads the Corporate Advisory department and the Employment Law and Intellectual Property Law specialty practice groups at Corpus.

Mabvuto's firm, formerly known as Corpus Globe, has been a member of Lex Africa, a network of leading law firms on the African continent. It is also a member of the World Services Group.

Mabvuto received his LL.B. in Law in 2000 from the University of Zambia, a practice certificate from the Zambia Institute of Advance Legal Education in 2002, a Post Graduate Diploma in Law from Lund University in Sweden and a Masters of Law in 2006 from the University of Nottingham in the United Kingdom. He is also a member of the Law Association of Zambia, SADC Lawyers Association, International Bar Association and London based Chartered Institute of Arbitrators.

E-mail address: msakala@corpus.co.zm

About the Book

Franchising in Zambia 2014: Legal and Business Considerations contains excerpts from the larger work, *Franchising in Africa 2014: Legal and Business Considerations.* Both books serve as practical, succinct, easy-to-use reference tools for lawyers, business people and academics to use in navigating the myriad laws and business issues impacting franchise arrangements on the African continent.

This book provides an overview of the franchise industry in Zambia and addresses the typical legal issues confronted when expanding a franchise system in Zambia. The larger work, *Franchising in Africa 2014: Legal and Business Considerations,* covers those laws governing franchising in fifteen other African countries – Angola, Botswana, Burundi, Cape Verde, Democratic Republic of Congo, Egypt, Ethiopia, Ghana, Kenya, Mozambique, Nigeria, Rwanda, South Africa, Tunisia and Zimbabwe.

In both books, an author, who is a legal expert in the designated jurisdiction, addresses the basic questions that a franchise lawyer would need to know to competently represent a client in expanding their franchise system to that country.

Each country chapter organizes a discussion of that country's laws under various headings and in a uniform format. Topics were sent to each country's author in the form of a questionnaire, and each author drafted responses to the questions presented. A general overview relating to the political and economic history of the country at the beginning of each chapter provides an initial context for the regulatory framework.[1]

---

[1] The source of information for these sections is the Central Intelligence Agency, https://www.cia.gov/library/publications/the-world-factbook/ (last visited November 3, 2013).

Apart from an overview of the legal framework for franchising, each book contains other articles and resources that should prove useful to those in the franchise industry.

The authors for each chapter are listed at the beginning of a chapter and their biographical information is listed in the previous section, *About the Editors and Authors*.

Readers should always consult with local counsel in the relevant jurisdiction instead of relying solely on the information contained in this book. The laws governing franchising are evolving and local counsel in Zambia are best positioned to provide timely, relevant advice applying the current law to the particular facts of a case.

Franchising in Zambia

Mabvuto Sakala

Corpus Legal Practitioners

Lusaka, Zambia

I.   Introduction

A.   Historical Background of Country

During the 1920s and 1930s, advances in mining spurred development and immigration to the territory of Northern Rhodesia. Its name was changed to Zambia upon independence from the United Kingdom in 1964. In the 1980s and 1990s, declining copper prices and a prolonged drought hurt the economy. Elections in 1991 brought an end to one-party rule under Kenneth Kaunda when Frederick Chiluba came into power with the Movement for Multi-party Democracy Party ("MMD"). At the end of his second term of office, Chiluba was succeeded by Levy Mwanawasa who was also a member of MMD. Mwanawasa was re-elected in 2006 in an election that was deemed free and fair. He died in the middle of his second term of office and was subsequently succeed by his Vice President Rupiah Banda, who won a special presidential election in October 2008. In October 2011, Zambia had elections in which the current President Michael Sata emerged victorious. These elections resulted in a transition in government from the MMD to the Patriotic Front ("PF") that for the most part was free, fair, and peaceful.

B.   Economy of the Country

Zambia's economy has experienced strong growth in recent years, with real GDP growth in 2005–08 at about 6% per year. Privatization of government-owned copper mines in the 1990s relieved the government from covering mammoth losses generated by the industry and greatly improved the chances for copper mining to return to profitability and spur economic growth. In fact, copper output has increased steadily since 2004 due to higher copper prices and foreign investment. In 2005, Zambia qualified for debt relief under the IMF's Highly Indebted Poor Country Initiative, consisting of approximately US$6 billion in debt relief. The decline in world commodity prices and demand hurt GDP growth in 2009, but a sharp rebound in copper prices and a bumper maize crop have helped Zambia begin to recover. Recently, Zambia was re-classified as a middle-income country by the World Bank and was assigned a B+ sovereign credit by two internationally recognized credit agencies, Standard and Poor's and Fitch.

C. Franchise Legal Overview

Under the Zambian law, there is no specific law that regulates franchise agreements or transactions. The franchise agreement is seen as a contractual agreement between the parties and thus contract law will govern such an agreement.

II. Regulatory Requirements

A. Pre-Sale Disclosure

Please describe any pre-sale franchise disclosure or similar requirements that may apply to franchise transactions.

No pre-sale franchise disclosure or similar requirements apply to franchise transactions under the laws of Zambia.

B. Governmental Approvals, Registrations, Filing Requirements

Please describe any necessary government approvals, registrations, or filing requirements that may apply to franchise transactions.

Zambia does not have any legislation that explicitly regulates franchises.

However, it is advisable to have a franchise agreement approved by the Competition and Consumer Protection Commission (the "Commission"). The Commission is a statutory body created by the *Competition and Consumer Protection Act No. 24 of 2010* (the "CCPA") to review the operations of markets in Zambia and the conditions of competition in these markets. Generally, the Act classifies as anti-competitive any category of agreement, decision or concerted practice that has as its object or effect, the prevention, restriction or distortion of competition to an appreciable extent in Zambia.

Under the CCPA, any enterprise that enters into an agreement that may have the effect of preventing, distorting or substantially lessening competition is required to obtain negative clearance from the Commission. Negative clearance is certification by the Commission that otherwise anti-competitive conduct can be allowed under conditions specified by the Commission. In addition, the CCPA provides for the enforceability of certain agreements that may be considered anti-competitive provided the agreements satisfy any of the exemption conditions listed under the Act.

The agreement may be exempted if is likely to contribute to:

(a)   maintaining or promoting exports from Zambia;

(b)   promoting or maintaining the efficient production, distribution or provision of goods and services;

(c)   promoting technical or economic progress in the production, distribution or provision of goods and services;

(d)   maintaining lower prices, higher quality or greater choice of goods and services for consumers;

(e)   promoting the competitiveness of micro and small business enterprises in Zambia; or

(f)   obtaining a benefit for the public which outweighs or would outweigh the lessening in competition that would result, or is likely to result from the competition.

The Commission may grant an exemption subject to such conditions and for such period as it considers appropriate. Should an application for exemption be rejected, the Commission is obliged to give reasons for rejecting an exemption, which reason presumably will be that the agreement does not qualify under any of the instances of exemption enumerated above.

There is no statutory period within which the Commission is required to revert to an applicant. The length of time to obtain approval will generally depend on administrative procedures within the Commission.

If exemption is obtained from the Commission, the terms of the franchise agreement will be rendered legally binding by the execution of the agreement, subject to its authentication if executed outside Zambia.

Further, if the franchise agreement relates to a trade name, services or goods that are registered with the Patents and Companies Registration Agency ("PACRA"), the franchise agreement will itself be required to be registered with PACRA

Apart from the provisions of the CCPA and the requirement to register a franchise agreement involving a registered trade name, services or goods, there are no other requirements for a franchise agreement to be registered, recorded or filed at any public office to render it legally binding.

C.   Limits of Fees and Typical Term of Franchise Agreement

Please describe any limits upon the nature and extent of fees and the term of a typical franchise agreement.

As an essentially contractual transaction, the nature and terms of the franchise agreement will be as determined by the parties thereto, conditional on the general requirement that the object of the agreement should not be illegal or against public policy.

III.   Currency

If all payments under a franchise agreement must be made in immediately available U.S. Dollars, please advise as to any restrictions, reporting requirements, or regulations concerning the exchange, repatriation, or remittance of U.S. Dollars.

Zambia does not have foreign exchange controls. It has a liberal foreign exchange market that operates through commercial banks and bureaux de change. However, *Statutory Instrument*

No. 33 of 2012 prohibits quoting, paying, demanding payment or receiving foreign currency as legal tender for goods, services or any other domestic transaction. A domestic transaction has been defined in *Statutory Instrument No. 78 of 2012* as one involving Zambian based counterparties within Zambia, in contrast to an international transaction which has been defined as a transaction involving a person or entity who is not resident in Zambia.

Thus, the prohibition of the use of foreign currency as legal tender applies only to those transactions between parties resident in Zambian but does not affect transactions in which one of the parties is not resident in Zambia.

Further, the *Bank of Zambia (Amendment) Act No. 1 of 2013* has now restricted the power of the Bank of Zambia (Central Bank) to only taking measures to monitor balance of payment transactions. In so doing, the Bank of Zambia may, to some extent, have the power to issue directives with respect to the mentioned transactions. Under the amendment, the Bank of Zambia in promoting the efficient operation of the foreign exchange system, may take measures to monitor:

(a)   foreign exchange inflows and outflows remitted;

(b)   imports and exports of goods and other inflows and outflows;

(c)   international transactions in services;

(d)   international transfers to or from non-residents;

(e)   profits or dividends received in respect of investments abroad;

(f)   borrowing and trade credits from non-residents;

(g)   investment in the form of equity and debt securities abroad;

(h)   receipts of both principal and interest on loans to non-residents; and

(i)   international money transfers into and out of Zambia.

This, to a fairly large extent, limits the powers of the Bank of Zambia to create formal standards, codes of conduct or rules with regard to the issue of restrictions on dealing in foreign exchange.

IV.   Taxes, Tariffs, and Duties

Please do not provide any in-depth comments on tax structuring. However, please provide your general comments on the typical amount of withholding tax that would apply and whether a "gross-up" provision contained in a franchise agreement would be enforceable in your country.

The position of the law in Zambia is that tax is chargeable from a source within or deemed to be within the Republic. Under the *Income Tax Act*, Chapter 323 of the Laws of Zambia, income is deemed to be from within the Republic if it arises from a royalty incurred in the production of income or in the carrying on of a business in the Republic or paid directly or indirectly out of funds derived from within the Republic.

In light of this, a franchisee in Zambia would be liable for withholding tax on royalties at the standard rate of 15% to resident recipients and 20% for payments to non-residents as of the 2013 financial year.

There are no restrictions under Zambia legislation that would prevent the insertion of a standard gross-up tax clause in an agreement; consequently, contracting parties are at liberty to have such a clause in their contract. Such a gross-up provision contained in a franchise agreement would be upheld as a matter of practice.

The tariffs and duties applicable will vary per franchise agreement depending on the subject matter of the tariffs. Zambia is a signatory to the *General Agreement on Tariffs and Trade* ("GATT") and its ancillary agreements. Therefore, its tariffs and duties are largely determined by its commitments under the GATT.

Zambia is a signatory to double taxation agreements with the following countries: Canada, Denmark, Finland, France, Germany, Holland, India, Ireland, Italy, Japan, Kenya, Norway, South Africa, Sweden, Tanzania, Uganda and the United Kingdom.

In addition, Zambia has double taxation agreements with Mauritius, Yugoslavia and Zimbabwe. However, to date, these agreements have not been ratified and as such cannot be relied on in Zambian courts.

V.   Trademarks

Please advise us as to whether there are any special requirements for granting a valid trademark license, including the use of a registered user agreement or a short trademark license agreement and any required filing of such an agreement with the trademark authorities.

The *Trademarks Act* (the "Act") does not specify any special requirements for granting a trademark license. In this regard, the basic principles of contract law apply. Trademark licensing is, however, a recognized way through which a trademark can be managed and protected in Zambia. Under the Act, a trademark owner can license third parties to do the acts that are covered by the exclusive rights of the trademark in relation to goods, that is, affixing the trademark on the goods, containers, packaging, and labels and using it in advertising, promotional activities, business papers and documents. The license can exclusive or non-exclusive.

Any person other than the proprietor of the trademark must apply to the Registrar of Trade Marks to be registered as the user of that trademark in Zambia.

The application for registration of a person as a registered user should be made by the proprietor and the registered user in writing. The application must be accompanied by information verified by statutory declaration relating to the relationship, existing or proposed, between the proprietor and the proposed registered owner, the goods for which registration is proposed, any conditions or restrictions proposed with respect to the characteristics of the goods and the period of the permitted use if limited in duration.

The Registrar of Trade Marks may register the proposed registered user, after considering the information furnished, and after being satisfied that, in the circumstances, the use of the trademark in relation to the proposed goods by the proposed registered user would not be contrary to the public interest. The Registrar may, however, refuse an application if it appears to him that the grant would facilitate trafficking in the trademark.

VI.   Restrictions on Transfer

Please advise as to whether there are any restrictions (1) on a franchisor to restrict transfers in a master franchisee, any interest in a master franchisee, or the assets of the master franchisee or (2) the ability of a master franchisee to control and/or restrict transfers of a subfranchisee's rights under a master franchise agreement, interest in the subfranchisee, or the assets of the subfranchisee.

As per Section II.B. above, any agreements restricting the acquisition of interests as between a franchisor and a master franchisee or any agreements as between a master franchisee and a subfranchisee must be approved by the Commission.   The Commission is likely to prohibit an agreement that has the effect of preventing, distorting or restricting competition or substantially lessening competition in a market for any goods or services unless an exemption for the restrictive agreement is obtained in accordance with the procedure outlined in Section II.B. above.

Regarding the transfer of assets, the parties may determine what restrictions will be placed on the transfer of assets but generally there are no restrictions on the transfer of property.   However, the *Property Transfer Tax Act*, Chapter 340 of the Laws of Zambia provides that whenever any property is transferred, there must be charged upon, and collected from, the person transferring such property, a property transfer tax, which rate is currently fixed at 5 percent of the realized value of the property. The definition of property here comprises any land in Zambia and any shares issued by a company incorporated in Zambia.

Accordingly, any transfer of shares or land whether as between the franchisor and the master franchisee or as between the master franchisee and sub franchisees may be subject to payment of property transfer tax.

VII. Termination

Please advise us as to any laws relating to termination in your country, such as agency laws, required indemnity provisions, notice or "good cause" requirements, or other laws affecting termination of a franchise agreement. Please describe.

Considering their contractual nature, franchise agreements are terminable by expiration of the term or by notice. In instances of change of legislation, the parties may consent to the continuation of the agreement in its executed form unless that change in legislation renders continued performance of the agreement illegal.

The *Interpretation and General Provisions Act*, Chapter 2 of the Laws of Zambia provides that the repeal of any written law will not affect any right, privilege, obligation or liability acquired, accrued or incurred under that law. However, where legislation is repealed and amended or replaced, the amending or replacing legislation may specifically provide for the effect of the change in legislation.

VIII. Governing Law, Jurisdiction, and Dispute Resolution

A.   Choice of Law of Foreign Jurisdiction

Please confirm whether the choice of law of a foreign jurisdiction would likely to be upheld under the law of the country, except for certain matters such as trademarks, bankruptcy, and competition matters, which we assume would be governed by the law in your country.

Parties are at liberty to choose the governing law of their agreements and there is no legal restriction pertaining to the choice of law by contracting parties. In practice, non-Zambian citizens tend to choose foreign law and it is not uncommon for parties to choose English law due to the fact that Zambia is a common law jurisdiction.

However, if the parties do not agree on which law will prevail, the common law principles dictate that the governing law will be that of the place where the agreement is performed. In determining the governing law, the court may also consider other factors such as intention of the parties, common usage and trade for that particular transaction, prior negotiations between the parties and the place of conclusion of the contract.

B. International Arbitration Dispute Resolution

Please confirm that a court in your country would honor an election of international arbitration dispute resolution, and therefore refuse to hear any disputes arising under a franchise agreement.

Courts in Zambia would honor an election of international arbitration dispute resolution subject to the provisions of the *Arbitration Act No. 19 of 2000* (the "Arbitration Act"). The Arbitration Act recognizes as binding arbitral awards issued under the auspices of the *Convention on the Recognition and Enforcement of Foreign Arbitral Awards* (the "New York Convention"), irrespective of the country in which it was made, upon application in writing to a competent court. In this regard, arbitral awards in Zambia are recognized and enforced under the *Geneva Convention on the Execution of Foreign Arbitral Awards* and the New York Convention.

Recognition or enforcement of a foreign arbitral award may however be refused if, at the request of the party against whom it is invoked, a party furnishes to the competent court where recognition or enforcement is sought, proof of any of the following, non-exclusive facts:

- a party to the arbitration agreement was under some incapacity;

- the agreement is not valid under the law to which the parties have subjected it or, failing any indication thereon, under the law of the country where the award was made;

- the party against whom the award is invoked was not given proper notice of the appointment of an arbitrator or of the arbitral proceedings or was otherwise unable to present its case; or

- the award has not yet become binding on the parties or has been set aside or suspended by a court of the country in which, or under the law of which, that award was made.

IX.   Non-Competition Provisions

If the franchise agreement prohibits the master franchisee from engaging in certain competitive activities during the term of the agreement, and for a 12-month period after the termination or expiration of the agreement, please comment on the enforceability of non-competition covenants in your country.

Non-compete covenants are essentially contractual and therefore subject to agreement as between the parties. The law in Zambia recognizes the enforceability of a non-compete clause provided the terms are reasonable. Where the term is considered unreasonable, the courts may be unwilling to enforce them for being unreasonable in restraint of trade. What is reasonable is determined on a case-to-case basis but the court may give consideration to factors such as the term of the covenant and the geographical area to which the covenant extends.

X.   Language Requirements

Does the law in your country require that a franchise agreement be translated into the local language in order to be enforceable between the parties?

There is no requirement under Zambian law that makes it a requirement for a franchise agreement to be translated into any local language for the purpose of enforceability as between the parties.

XI. Other Significant Matters

Please advise as to whether there are any significant matters not addressed above of which a franchisor should be aware in connection with its entering into a franchise agreement in your country.

In the event that the franchise agreement is executed outside of Zambia, it will only be enforceable in Zambia if it is authenticated in accordance with the *Authentication of Documents Act*.

Under the *Authentication of Documents Act*, in order for any document executed outside Zambia to be enforceable in Zambia, the document must be authenticated in the manner prescribed. Documents executed in the United Kingdom are sufficiently authenticated if they are executed before a notary public and signed and duly sealed by such notary public. In the case of an execution of documents from any other jurisdiction outside Zambia other than the United Kingdom, the signature and seal of the notary public must be certified by the consular office in Zambia of that foreign jurisdiction.

Thus, a franchise agreement executed outside of the country will have to be authenticated if it is to have legal efficacy in Zambia.

- *Please provide any insight as to any proposed franchise specific legislation that may be under consideration in your jurisdiction.*

There is currently no franchise association in Zambia and there is no franchise-specific legislation being considered currently in the country.

- *Please provide a sample of the franchised brands that operate in your country.*

  - Kentucky Fried Chicken (KFC)
  - Subway

Bibliography of International Franchise Resources

Kendal H. Tyre, Jr., Diana Vilmenay-Hammond, Pierce Haesung Han, Courtney L. Lindsay II, and Keri McWilliams

Nixon Peabody LLP

Washington, D.C.

I.   General International Resources

Mark Abell, Gary R. Duvall, and Andrea Oricchio Kirsh, *International Franchise Legislation* B1, ABA FORUM ON FRANCHISING (1996)

Kathleen C. Anderson and Anthony M. Stiegler, *Put Muscle in Your Marks: Enforcing Intellectual Property Rights* W14, ABA FORUM ON FRANCHISING (1995)

Richard M. Asbill and Jane W. LaFranchi, *International Franchise Sales Laws—A Survey* W7, ABA FORUM ON FRANCHISING (2005)

Jeffery A. Brimer, Alison C. McElroy, and John Pratt, *Going International: What Additional Restraints Will You Face?* W4, ABA FORUM ON FRANCHISING (2011)

Michael G. Brennan, Alexander Konigsberg, and Philip F. Zeidman, *Globetrotting: A Workshop on International Franchising* 10/W8, ABA FORUM ON FRANCHISING (1994)

Michael G. Brennan, Alexander Konigsberg, and Philip F. Zeidman, *Globetrotting: Strategies for Launching U.S. Franchisors Abroad* 2/P2, ABA FORUM ON FRANCHISING (1994)

Christopher P. Bussert and Jennifer Dolman, *Regaining Your Trademark After Abandonment or Misappropriation* W7, ABA FORUM ON FRANCHISING (2011)

Ronald T. Coleman and Linda K. Stevens, *Trade Secrets and Confidential Information: Rights and Remedies* W2, ABA FORUM ON FRANCHISING (2000)

Finola Cunningham, *Commerce Department Helps Franchisors Go Global*, in FRANCHISING WORLD 63 (Dec. 2005)

Michael R. Daigle and Alex S. Konigsberg, *Meeting Off-Shore Disclosure and Contract Requirements* F/W13, ABA FORUM ON FRANCHISING (1992)

Jennifer Dolman, Robert A. Lauer, and Lawrence M. Weinberg, *Structuring International Master Franchise Relationships for Success and Responding When Things Go Awry* W22, ABA FORUM ON FRANCHISING (2007)

Gary R. Duvall, Paul Jones, and Jane LaFranchi, *Planning for the International Enforcement of Franchise Agreements* W6, ABA FORUM ON FRANCHISING (1999)

William Edwards, *International Expansion: Do Opportunities Outweigh Challenges?* in FRANCHISING WORLD (February 2008)

George J. Eydt and Stuart Hershman, *Bringing a Foreign Franchise System to the United States* W9, ABA FORUM ON FRANCHISING (2009)

William A. Finkelstein and Louis T. Pirkey, *International Trademarks* W15, ABA FORUM ON FRANCHISING (1991)

William A. Finkelstein, *Protecting Trademarks Internationally: Current Strategies and Developments* B3, ABA FORUM ON FRANCHISING (1996)

Stephen Giles, Lou H. Jones, and Lawrence Weinberg, *Negotiating and Documenting Complex International Franchise Agreements* W21, ABA FORUM ON FRANCHISING (2006)

Steven M. Goldman, Stephen Giles, Marc Israel, and Stanley Wong, *Competition Round Up from Around the World* LB2, ABA FORUM ON FRANCHISING (2004)

David C. Gryce and E. Lynn Perry, *Trademarks and Copyrights in the International Arena* 6/W4, ABA FORUM ON FRANCHISING (1993)

Kenneth S. Kaplan, Andrew P. Loewinger, and Penelope J. Ward, *System Standards in International Franchising* W14, ABA FORUM ON FRANCHISING (2005)

Edward Levitt and Jorge Mondragon, *A Survey of International Legal Traps and How to Avoid Them—Beyond the Franchise Laws* W20, ABA FORUM ON FRANCHISING (2007)

Ned Levitt, Kendal H. Tyre, and Penny Ward, *The Impossible Dream: Controlling Your International Franchise System* W4, ABA FORUM ON FRANCHISING (2010)

Michael K. Lindsey and Andrew P. Loewinger, *International (Non-U.S.) Franchise Disclosure Requirements* W9, ABA FORUM ON FRANCHISING (2002)

Andrew P. Loewinger and John Pratt, *Recent Changes and Trends in International Franchise Laws* W4, ABA FORUM ON FRANCHISING (2008)

Andrew P. Loewinger and Thomas M. Pitegoff, *Avoiding the Long Arm of the Law in International Franchising: Issues and Approaches* W8, ABA FORUM ON FRANCHISING (1995)

Craig J. Madson and Katherine C. Spelman, *Similarity and Confusion in the Intellectual Property Arena* W11, ABA FORUM ON FRANCHISING (1997)

Christopher A. Nowak, John Pratt, and Carl E. Zwisler, *Franchising Internationally with Countries with Opaque Legal Systems* W20, ABA FORUM ON FRANCHISING (2006)

E. Lynn Perry and John L. Sullivan Jr., *Trademark Compliance and Enforcement Techniques* E/W12, ABA FORUM ON FRANCHISING (1992)

Marcel Portmann, *Franchising Sector Proves Global Reach*, in FRANCHISING WORLD (January 2007)

John Pratt and Luiz Henrique O. do Amaral, *Civil Law for Common Law Practitioners (or How to Draft an Agreement for Use Overseas)* W4, ABA FORUM ON FRANCHISING (2002)

Kirk W. Reilly, Robert F. Salkowski and Geoffrey B. Shaw, *Determining the Rules of Engagement in Litigation Here and Abroad* W5, ABA FORUM ON FRANCHISING (2008)

Catherine Riesterer and Frank Zaid, *Basics of International Franchising* L/B2, ABA FORUM ON FRANCHISING (1997)

W. Andrew Scott and Christopher N. Wormald, *Stranger in a Strange Land: Contrasting Franchising in International Expansion* W2, ABA FORUM ON FRANCHISING (2003)

Donald Smith and Erik Wulff, *International Franchising: The Unraveling of an International Franchise Relationship* 15/W13, ABA FORUM ON FRANCHISING (1993)

Frank Zaid, Pamela Mills, and Michael Santa Maria, *Essential Issues in International Franchising* LB/1, ABA FORUM ON FRANCHISING (2001)

II.   African Resources

Joyce G. Mazero and J. Perry Maisonneuve, *Franchising in the Middle East and North Africa* W2, ABA FORUM ON FRANCHISING (2009)

Kendal H. Tyre, Jr. and Diana Vilmenay-Hammond, *Franchise World: A Burgeoning Middle Class Spurs Franchise Investment in Africa*, MINORITY BUSINESS ENTREPRENEUR (November 2012)

Kendal H. Tyre, Jr., *IP Protection May Promote Additional Franchise Growth in Africa*, NIXON PEABODY LLP: FRANCHISING BUSINESS & LAW ALERT (September 2012)

Kendal H. Tyre, Jr., *Market Potential for Franchising in Africa*, NIXON PEABODY LLP: FRANCHISING BUSINESS & LAW ALERT (June 2011)

Kendal H. Tyre, Jr. and Courtney L. Lindsay, II, *Continued Growth of Franchising in Africa*, NIXON PEABODY LLP: FRANCHISE LAW ALERT (April 2013)

Kendal H. Tyre, Jr. and Courtney L. Lindsay, II, *Pan African Franchise Federation Holds Inaugural Meeting*, NIXON PEABODY LLP: AFRICA ALERT (June 2013)

Kendal H. Tyre, Jr. and Courtney L. Lindsay, II, *White House Encouraging Private Investment and Transparency in Sub-Saharan Africa*, NIXON PEABODY LLP: AFRICA ALERT (August 2012)

Kendal H. Tyre, Jr. and Diana Vilmenay-Hammond, *African Economic Growth Impacts Franchising on the Continent*, NIXON PEABODY LLP: FRANCHISE LAW ALERT (July 2012)

Kendal H. Tyre, Jr. and Diana Vilmenay-Hammond, *Franchising in Africa*, in FRANCHISING WORLD (August 2013)

John Sotos and Sam Hall, *African Franchising: Cross-Continent Momentum*, in FRANCHISING WORLD (June 2007)

A.   Angola

João Afonso Fialho, *Franchising in Angola*, in FRANCHISING IN AFRICA: LEGAL AND BUSINESS CONSIDERATIONS 91-105 (Kendal H. Tyre, Jr. & Diana Vilmenay-Hammond eds. 2012)

B.   Botswana

Bonzo Makgalemele, *Franchising in Botswana*, in FRANCHISING IN AFRICA: LEGAL AND BUSINESS CONSIDERATIONS 107-117 (Kendal H. Tyre, Jr. & Diana Vilmenay-Hammond eds. 2012)

C.   Cape Verde

João Afonso Fialho, *Franchising in Cape Verde*, in FRANCHISING IN AFRICA: LEGAL AND BUSINESS CONSIDERATIONS 119-132 (Kendal H. Tyre, Jr. & Diana Vilmenay-Hammond eds. 2012)

D.   Egypt

Girgis Abd El-Shahid, *Franchising in Eqypt*, in FRANCHISING IN AFRICA: LEGAL AND BUSINESS CONSIDERATIONS 133-142 (Kendal H. Tyre, Jr. & Diana Vilmenay-Hammond eds. 2012)

A. Safaa El Din El Oteifi, *Egypt*, in INTERNATIONAL FRANCHISING EGY/1 (Dennis Campbell gen. ed. 2011)

E.   Ethiopia

Yohannes Assefa and Biset Beyene Molla, *Franchising in Ethiopia*, in FRANCHISING IN AFRICA: LEGAL AND BUSINESS CONSIDERATIONS 143-157 (Kendal H. Tyre, Jr. & Diana Vilmenay-Hammond eds. 2012)

Kendal H. Tyre, Jr., Yohannes Assefa and Getachew Mengistie Alemu, *New Intellectual Property Regulation Requires Scramble to Protect Marks in Ethiopia*, NIXON PEABODY LLP: AFRICA ALERT (October 2013)

F.   Ghana

Divine K.D. Letsa and Hawa Tejansie Ajei, *Franchising in Ghana*, in FRANCHISING IN AFRICA: LEGAL AND BUSINESS CONSIDERATIONS 159-167 (Kendal H. Tyre, Jr. & Diana Vilmenay-Hammond eds. 2012)

G.   Libya

Kendal H. Tyre, Jr. & Diana Vilmenay-Hammond, *First U.S. Franchise Opens in Libya*, NIXON PEABODY LLP: AFRICA ALERT (August 2012)

H.   Mozambique

Diogo Xavier da Cunha, *Franchising in Mozambique*, in FRANCHISING IN AFRICA: LEGAL AND BUSINESS CONSIDERATIONS 169-182 (Kendal H. Tyre, Jr. & Diana Vilmenay-Hammond eds. 2012)

I.   Nigeria

Theo Emuwa and Bimbola Fowler-Ekar, *Franchising in Nigeria*, in FRANCHISING IN AFRICA: LEGAL AND BUSINESS CONSIDERATIONS 183-198 (Kendal H. Tyre, Jr. & Diana Vilmenay-Hammond eds. 2012)

Kendal H. Tyre, Jr. and Theo Emuwa, *Nigerian Franchising: Making Your Way Through the Thicket*, NIXON PEABODY LLP: FRANCHISE LAW ALERT (June 2005)

J.   South Africa

Eugene Honey, *Franchising and the New Consumer Protection Bill*, BOWMAN GILFILLAN (March 2008)

Eugene Honey, *Franchising and the Consumer Protection Bill*, BOWMAN GILFILLAN (May 2008)

Eugene Honey, *Pitfalls and Difficulties with the CPA*, ADAMS & ADAMS (March 2013)

Eugene Honey, *Disclosure is Compulsory*, ADAMS & ADAMS (May 2013)

Eugene Honey and Wim Alberts, *Fundamental Consumer Rights: The Right to Equality*, BOWMAN GILFILLAN (March 2009)

Eugene Honey and Wim Alberts, *The Reach of the Consumer Protection Bill: The Final*, BOWMAN GILFILLAN (March 2009)

Eugene Honey, *South Africa*, in GETTING THE DEAL THROUGH: FRANCHISE (2013) 172-178 (Philip F. Zeidman ed. 2013)

Taswell Papier, *Franchising in South Africa*, in FRANCHISING IN AFRICA: LEGAL AND BUSINESS CONSIDERATIONS 199-224 (Kendal H. Tyre, Jr. & Diana Vilmenay-Hammond eds. 2012)

Kendal H. Tyre, Jr., *A New Legal Landscape for Franchising in South Africa*, NIXON PEABODY LLP: FRANCHISING BUSINESS & LAW ALERT (September 2009)

K.　Tunisia

Yessine Ferah, *Franchising in Tunisia*, in FRANCHISING IN AFRICA: LEGAL AND BUSINESS CONSIDERATIONS 225-245 (Kendal H. Tyre, Jr. & Diana Vilmenay-Hammond eds. 2012)

Kendal H. Tyre, Jr., Diana Vilmenay-Hammond, and Yessine Ferah, *New Franchise Legislation in Tunisia*, NIXON PEABODY LLP: FRANCHISE LAW ALERT (September 2010)

L.　Zambia

Mabvuto Sakala, *Franchising in Zambia*, in FRANCHISING IN AFRICA: LEGAL AND BUSINESS CONSIDERATIONS 247-255 (Kendal H. Tyre, Jr. & Diana Vilmenay-Hammond eds. 2012)